DOILIES
in Color™

DOILIES in Color™

contents

DOILIES *in Color*

Gardenias

Gardenias, best known for their fragrant white flowers and sweet smell, stand for love, purity and joy. Because marriage symbolizes love and purity, gardenias are often used in wedding celebrations. This doily would make the perfect addition to any wedding. Stitch to match the colors of the wedding, or stitch in traditional white.

Gardenias

DESIGN BY **JOSIE RABIER**

SKILL LEVEL

INTERMEDIATE

FINISHED SIZE
26 inches in diameter

MATERIALS
- Size 10 crochet cotton:
  650 yds aqua
- Size 7/1.65mm steel crochet hook
  or size needed to obtain gauge
- Starch

GAUGE
Rnds 1–3 = 2 inches in diameter;
  2 shell rnds = 1 inch

PATTERN NOTES
Chain-3 at beginning of round counts as first
  double crochet unless otherwise stated.

Join rounds with slip stitch as indicated unless
  otherwise stated.

SPECIAL STITCHES
Shell: (3 dc, ch 3, 3 dc) in indicated st or ch sp.

Beginning shell (beg shell): Sl st in indicated st or
  ch sp, ch 3, (2 dc, ch 3, 3 dc) in same st or ch sp.

6-double treble crochet decrease (6-dtr dec):
  Keeping last lp of each st on hook, 2 **dtr** (see
  Stitch Guide) in next tr (3 lps on hook), dtr in
  each of next 2 tr (5 lps on hook), 2 dtr in next tr
  (7 lps on hook), yo, draw lp through all lps on
  hook, ch 1.

DOILY

Rnd 1 (RS): Ch 5, **join** (*see Pattern Notes*) in 5th ch from hook to form ring, **ch 3** (*see Pattern Notes*), 23 dc in ring, join in 3rd ch of beg ch-3. (*24 dc*)

Rnd 2: Ch 3, dc in next dc, ch 2, [dc in each of next 2 dc, ch 2] around, join in 3rd ch of beg ch-3.

Rnd 3: Ch 3, dc in next dc, ch 3, [dc in each of next 2 dc, ch 3] around, join in 3rd ch of beg ch-3.

Rnd 4: Ch 3, dc in same ch as beg ch-3, 2 dc in next dc, *sk next ch-3 sp, 2 dc in each of next 2 dc, ch 5, sk next ch-3 sp**, 2 dc in each of next 2 dc, rep from * around, ending last rep at **, join in 3rd ch of beg ch-3. (*48 dc, 6 ch-5 sps*)

Rnd 5: Ch 3, dc in each of next 2 dc, *sk next 2 dc, dc in each of next 3 dc, ch 5, sl st in next ch-5 sp, ch 5**, dc in each of next 3 dc, rep from * around, ending last rep at **, join in 3rd ch of beg ch-3. (*36 dc, 12 ch-5 sps*)

Rnd 6: Ch 3, dc in next dc, *sk next 2 dc, dc in each of next 2 dc, [ch 5, sl st in next ch-5 sp] twice, ch 5**, dc in each of next 2 dc, rep from * around, ending last rep at **, join in 3rd ch of beg ch-3. (*24 dc, 18 ch-5 sps*)

Rnd 7: Ch 3, *sk next 2 dc, dc in next dc, [ch 5, sl st in next ch-5 sp] 3 times, ch 5**, dc in next dc, rep from * around, ending last rep at **, join in 3rd ch of beg ch-3, sl st in 3rd ch of next ch-5 sp. (*12 dc, 24 ch-5 sps*)

Rnd 8: Ch 8 (*counts as first dc, ch-5*), dc in same sp as beg ch-8, *[(dc, ch 5, dc) in 3rd ch of next ch-5 sp] 3 times, ch 3, sk next 2 dc**, (dc, ch 5, dc) in 3rd ch of next ch-5 sp, rep from * around, ending last rep at **, join in 3rd ch of beg ch-8.

Rnd 9: Sl st in next ch-5 sp, ch 3, 4 dc in same ch sp as beg ch-3, *5 dc in each of next 3 ch-5 sps, 5 dc in next ch-3 sp**, 5 dc in next ch-5 sp, rep from * around, ending last rep at **, join in 3rd ch of beg ch-3. (*150 dc*)

Rnd 10: Ch 3, dc in next dc, *(dc, ch 5, dc) in next dc**, dc in each of next 4 dc, rep from * around, ending last rep at **, dc in each of last 2 dc, join in 3rd ch of beg ch-3.

Rnd 11: Sl st in next ch-5 sp, **beg shell** (*see Special Stitches*) in same ch-5 sp, **shell** (*see Special Stitches*) in each rem ch-5 sp around, join in 3rd ch of beg ch-3. (*30 shells*)

Rnd 12: Sl st in next ch-3 sp, beg shell in same ch-3 sp, shell in each ch-3 sp around, join in 3rd ch of beg ch-3. Fasten off.

FIRST FLOWER

Rnd 1: Ch 4, 15 dc in 4th ch from hook (*beg 3 sk chs count as first dc*), join in 4th ch of beg ch-4. (*16 dc*)

Rnd 2: [Ch 3, 6 dc in same dc as beg ch-3, sk next dc, sl st in next dc] 8 times. (*8 petals*)

Rnd 3: Holding petals forward and working behind petals in sk dc of previous rnd, sl st in next sk dc, [ch 5, sl st in next sk dc of previous rnd] around, sl st in same dc as beg ch-5, join in next ch-5 sp. (*8 ch-5 sps*)

Rnd 4: Beg shell in same ch-5 sp as join, 3 dc in next ch-5 sp, ch 1, sl st in ch-3 sp of any shell on rnd 12 of Doily, ch 1, 3 dc in same ch-5 sp of Flower, 3 dc in next ch-5 sp, ch 1, sl st in ch-3 sp of next shell on rnd 12 of Doily, ch 1, 3 dc in same ch-5 sp of Flower, shell in each of next 5 rem ch-5 sps of Flower, join in 3rd ch of beg ch-3. Fasten off.

continued on page 40

DOILIES *in Color*

Pink Sunset

Envision a southwestern desert sunset skimming an array of desert blooms with it's pinkish orangish hue. Frame and display **Pink Sunset** to picture the moment the trailing edge of the Sun's disk disappears below the horizon in the west, creating intense orange and red colors.

Pink Sunset

DESIGN BY **CAROL ALEXANDER**

SKILL LEVEL

■■■□ INTERMEDIATE

FINISHED SIZE
12 inches in diameter

MATERIALS
- Size 10 crochet cotton:
  1 ball coral
- Size 7/1.65mm steel crochet hook
  or size needed to obtain gauge
- Tapestry needle

GAUGE
Rnds 1–3 (center flower) = 2½ inches

Take time to check gauge.

PATTERN NOTES
Weave in loose ends as work progresses.

Join rounds with slip stitch as indicated
unless otherwise stated.

SPECIAL STITCHES
Small picot (sm picot): Ch 3, sl st in 3rd ch
from hook.

Large picot (lg picot): Ch 4, sl st in top of last
dc made.

Shell: (4 dc, ch 2, 4 dc) in indicated st.

3-treble crochet cluster (3-tr cl): Keeping last lp
of each st on hook, work 3 tr in indicated st
or sp, yo, draw through all lps on hook.

V-stitch (V-st): (Dc, ch 2, dc) in indicated st
or sp.

Joining small picot (joining sm picot): Ch 1, sl st in
indicated ch sp on rnd 8 of Doily, ch 1, sl st in
first ch-1 of joining sm picot.

DOILY
Rnd 1 (RS): Ch 2, 8 sc in 2nd ch from hook, **join**
(*see Pattern Notes*) in beg sc. (*8 sc*)

Rnd 2: Ch 1, sc in same st as beg ch-1, ch 4,
[sc in next sc, ch 4] 7 times, join in beg sc.
(*8 ch-4 sps*)

Rnd 3: Sl st in next ch-4 sp, *(ch 4, **3-tr cl**—*see
Special Stitches*, **sm picot**—*see Special Stitches*,
3-tr cl, ch 4, sl st) in same ch-4 sp as sl st (*petal*),
sl st in next ch-4 sp, rep from * around, join in
base of beg ch-4. (*8 petals*)

Rnd 4: Sl st in each of next 4 chs, sl st in sm picot
of first petal, ch 1, sc in same place as beg ch-1,
ch 8, [sc in next sm picot of next petal, ch 8] 7
times, join in beg sc.

Rnd 5: Ch 1, *6 sc in next ch-8 sp, ch 12, **turn**,
sl st in first ch to form ring, ch 1, **turn**, (sc, hdc,
7 dc, **lg picot**—*see Special Stitches*, 7 dc, hdc,
sc) in ring just made, sl st at base of ring, 6 sc in
same ch-8 sp, rep from * around, join in beg sc.
Fasten off. (*8 rings*)

Rnd 6: Join in 3rd dc to left of any lg picot, ch 7
(*counts as first tr, ch-3*), *tr in 3rd dc to right of
lg picot on next ring, ch 3, tr in next dc, ch 10,
tr in 2nd dc to left of same lg picot, ch 3**, tr in
next dc, ch 3, rep from * around, ending last rep
at **, join in 4th ch of beg ch-7.

Rnd 7: Ch 1, *[sc in next ch-3 sp, ch 4] twice, **shell** *(see Special Stitches)* in center of next ch-10 sp, ch 4, sc in next ch-3 sp**, ch 4, rep from * around, ending last rep at **, ch 1, join with dc in beg sc.

Rnd 8: Ch 1, sc in sp formed at joining, *ch 3, sc in next ch-4 sp, ch 2, **V-st** *(see Special Stitches)* in next ch-4 sp, ch 4, shell in ch-2 sp of next shell, ch 4, V-st in next ch-4 sp, ch 2 *(scallop)***, sc in next ch-4 sp, rep from * around, ending last rep at **, join in beg sc. Fasten off. *(8 scallops)*

FLOWER RING
MAKE 8.
Rnds 1 & 2: Rep rnds 1 & 2 of Doily.

Note: Smooth and flatten all flower petals at end of rnd 3.

Rnd 3: Sl st in next ch-4 sp, work rem row as follows:

A. *(Ch 4, 3-tr cl, sm picot, 3-tr cl, ch 4, sl st) in same ch-4 sp *(petal)*, sl st in next ch-4 sp, rep from * 4 times;

B. ch 4, 3-tr cl in next ch-4 sp, **joining sm picot** *(see Special Stitches)* in ch sp of first V-st of Scallop on rnd 8 of Doily, (3-tr cl, ch 4, sl st) in same ch-4 sp on Flower as previous 3-tr cl *(joined petal)*, sl st in next ch-4 sp;

C. ch 4, 3-tr cl in next ch-4 sp, joining sm picot in next ch sp of Scallop on rnd 8 of Doily, (3-tr cl, ch 4, sl st) in same ch-4 sp on Flower as previous 3-tr cl *(joined petal)*, sl st in next ch-4 sp;

D. ch 4, 3-tr cl in next ch-4 sp, joining sm picot in ch sp of last V-st of next Scallop on rnd 8 of Doily, (3-tr cl, ch 4, sl st) in same ch-4 sp on Flower as previous 3-tr cl *(joined petal)*, join in base of beg ch-4. *(8 petals)*

EDGING
Join in ch-2 sp of any shell on rnd 8, ch 3 *(counts as first dc)*, (dc, lg picot, 2 dc) in same sp as beg ch-3, *ch 2, [sc in picot on next free petal of Flower, (ch 1, sm picot) 3 times, ch 2] 4 times, sc in next picot on next petal, ch 2**, (2 dc, lg picot, 2 dc) in ch-2 sp of next shell, rep from * around, ending last rep at **, join in 3rd ch of beg ch-3. Fasten off.

FINISHING
Block Doily to size. ∎

DOILIES *in Color*

Marigolds

Marigolds are a versatile flower. Known as the "Herb of the Sun" they are symbolic of passion and creativity; when planted in your garden, the scent of a marigold will ward off insects and bugs. This Marigold doily is the perfect accent to add texture to a pillow or a patio table at your next party.

Marigolds

DESIGN BY **JOSIE RABIER**

FINISHED SIZE
13 inches in diameter

MATERIALS
- Size 10 crochet cotton:
  350 yds gold
- Size 7/1.65mm steel crochet hook
  or size needed to obtain gauge
- Starch

GAUGE
8 dc = 1 inch; rnds 1 and 2 = 1¾ inches
  in diameter

Take time to check gauge.

PATTERN NOTES
Weave in loose ends as work progresses.

Join rounds with slip stitch unless
  otherwise stated.

Chain-3 at beginning of row or round counts as
  first double crochet unless otherwise stated.

SPECIAL STITCHES
5-double crochet popcorn (5-dc pc): Work 5 dc
  in indicated st or sp, drop lp from hook, insert
  hook in first dc, place dropped lp on hook, pull
  through first st.

Split double crochet decrease (split dc dec):
  Keeping last lp of each st on hook, dc in each of
  next 2 sts, sk next 2 sts, dc in each of next 3 sts,
  yo, draw lp through all lps on hook, ch 1.

CENTER

Rnd 1 (RS): Ch 8, **join** (*see Pattern Notes*) in 8th ch from hook to form ring, **ch 3** (*see Pattern Notes*), 23 dc in ring, join in 3rd ch of beg ch-3. (*24 dc*)

Rnd 2: Ch 3, dc in each of next 2 dc, ch 3, [dc in each of next 3 dc, ch 3] around, join in 3rd ch of beg ch-3.

Rnd 3: Ch 3, *3 dc in next dc, dc in next dc, ch 3, sk next ch-3 sp**, dc in next dc, rep from * around, ending last rep at **, join in 3rd ch of beg ch-3. (*40 dc*)

Rnd 4: Ch 3, dc in same st as beg ch-3, *dc in each of next 3 dc, 2 dc in next dc, ch 3, sk next ch-3 sp**, 2 dc in next dc, rep from * around, ending last rep at **, join in 3rd ch of beg ch-3. (*56 dc*)

Rnd 5: Ch 3, dc in each of next 6 dc, *ch 3, sk next ch-3 sp**, dc in each of next 7 dc, rep from * around, ending last rep at **, join in 3rd ch of beg ch-3.

Rnd 6: Ch 3, dc in each of next 2 dc, *(dc, ch 5, dc) in next dc, dc in each of next 3 dc, ch 3, sk next ch-3 sp**, dc in each of next 3 dc, rep from * around, ending last rep at **, join in 3rd ch of beg ch-3. (*64 dc*)

Rnd 7: Sl st across to first dc of next 4-dc group, ch 3, dc in each of next 3 dc, *sk next ch-3 sp, dc in each of next 4 dc, ch 5, sl st in next ch-5 sp, ch 5**, dc in each of next 4 dc, rep from * around, ending last rep at **, join in 3rd ch of beg ch-3.

Rnd 8: Ch 3, dc in each of next 2 dc, *sk next 2 dc, dc in each of next 3 dc, [ch 5, sl st in next ch-5 sp] twice, ch 5**, dc in each of next 3 dc, rep from * around, ending last rep at **, join in 3rd ch of beg ch-3. (*48 dc*)

Rnd 9: Ch 3, dc in next dc, *sk next 2 dc, dc in each of next 2 dc, ch 3, sl st in next ch-5 sp, (**5-dc pc**—*see Special Stitches*, {ch 5, 5-dc pc} 3 times) in next ch-5 sp, sl st in next ch-5 sp, ch 3**, dc in each of next 2 dc, rep from * around, ending last rep at **, join in 3rd ch of beg ch-3. (*32 dc, 32 pc*)

Rnd 10: Ch 3, *sk next 2 dc, dc in next dc, ch 3, (5-dc pc, ch 5, 5-dc pc) in next ch-5 sp, (5-dc pc, {ch 5, 5-dc pc} 3 times) in next ch-5 sp, (5-dc pc, ch 5, 5-dc pc) in next ch-5 sp, ch 3, sk next ch-3 sp**, dc in next dc, rep from * around, ending last rep at **, join in 3rd ch of beg ch-3. (*64 pc, 16 dc*)

Rnd 11: Sl st in next dc, *ch 3, sk next ch-3 sp, 7 dc in next ch-5 sp, [7 tr in next ch-5 sp] 3 times, 7 dc in next ch-5 sp, ch 3, sk next ch-3 sp**, sl st in each of next 2 dc, rep from * around, ending last rep at **, sl st in next dc. Fasten off. (*112 dc, 168 tr*)

FIRST LEAF

Row 1 (RS): Sk tr sts, join in first dc to the left of tr groups, ch 3, dc in each of next 6 dc, sk next ch-3 sp, dc in each of next 7 dc, turn. (*14 dc*)

Row 2 (WS): Ch 3, dc in each of next 5 dc, sk next 2 dc, dc in each of next 6 dc, turn. (*12 dc*)

Row 3: Ch 3, dc in each of next 4 dc, sk next 2 dc, dc in each of next 5 dc, turn. (*10 dc*)

Row 4: Ch 3, dc in each of next 3 dc, sk next 2 dc, dc in each of next 4 dc, turn. (*8 dc*)

Row 5: Ch 2, **split dc dec** (*see Special Stitches*). Fasten off.

LEAVES 2-8

Rows 1–5: Rep rows 1–5 of First Leaf.

FIRST PETAL GROUP

Row 1 (RS): Join in first tr of any tr group on rnd 11, *ch 7, **tr dec** (*see Stitch Guide*) in next 5 sts, ch 1 to lock, ch 7**, sl st in each of next 2 tr, rep from * twice, ending last rep at **, ch 1, sl st in next tr. Fasten off.

PETAL GROUPS 2-8

Row 1: Rep row 1 of First Petal Group.

FINISHING

Starch lightly and press. ∎

DOILIES *in Color*

Irish Rose

As written by Chancellor "Chauncey" Olcott in 1899 for his production *A Romance of Athlone*, "My wild Irish Rose, the sweetest flower that grows. You may search everywhere, but none can compare with my wild Irish Rose." This delicate Irish Rose doily with it's picot trim is a classic and timeless design that cannot be compared.

Irish Rose

DESIGN BY **DOROTHY DRAKE**

SKILL LEVEL

INTERMEDIATE

FINISHED SIZE
16 inches in diameter

MATERIALS
- Size 10 crochet cotton:
  300 yds ecru
- Size 8/1.50mm steel crochet hook
  or size needed to obtain gauge
- Starch

GAUGE
10 sc = 1 inch; rnds 1–8 of rose = 2 inches
  in diameter

Take time to check gauge.

PATTERN NOTES
Weave in loose ends as work progresses.

Join rounds with slip stitch as indicated
unless otherwise stated.

SPECIAL STITCHES
Picot: Ch 4, sl st in first ch
of ch-4.

V-stitch (V-st): (Dc, ch
3, dc) in indicated st.

Beginning V-stitch
(beg V-st): Ch 6
(counts as dc and
ch-3), dc in same st
as beg ch-6.

Beginning picot (beg
picot): Ch 7, sl st in
4th ch from hook.

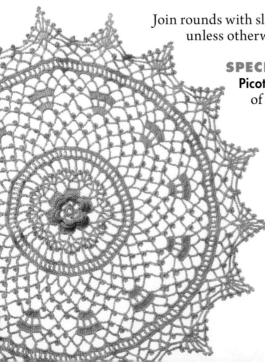

Chain-3 picot (ch-3 picot): Ch 3, sl st in first ch of
ch-3.

Chain-5 picot (ch-5 picot): Ch 5, sl st in first ch of
ch-5.

DOILY
Rnd 1 (RS): Ch 5, **join** (see Pattern Notes) in 5th
ch from hook to form ring, ch 1, 12 sc in ring,
join in beg sc. (12 sc)

Rnd 2: Ch 1, sc in same sc as beg ch-1, ch 4, sk
next sc, [sc in next sc, ch 4, sk next sc] around,
join in beg sc. (6 ch-4 sps)

Rnd 3: Ch 1, (sc, hdc, 3 dc, hdc, sc) in next ch-4
sp (petal) and in each rem ch-4 sp around, join
in beg sc. (6 petals)

Rnd 4: Working behind petals, [ch 4, sl st
between next 2 petals] around, sl st in same st
as beg ch-4. (6 ch-4 sps)

Rnd 5: Ch 1, (sc, hdc, 5 dc, hdc, sc) in next ch-4
sp (petal) and in each rem ch-4 sp around, join
in beg sc. (6 petals)

Rnd 6: Working behind petals, [ch 5, sl st
between next 2 petals] around, sl st in same st
as beg ch-5. (6 ch-5 sps)

Rnd 7: Ch 1, (sc, hdc, 8 dc, hdc, sc) in next ch-5
sp (petal) and in each rem ch-5 sp around, join
in beg sc. (6 petals)

Rnd 8: Sl st in each of next 3 sts, **beg V-st** (see
Special Stitches), ch 3, sk next 4 dc, **V-st** (see
Special Stitches) in next dc, ch 3, *V-st in 2nd dc
of next petal, ch 3, sk next 4 dc, V-st in next dc,
ch 3, rep from * around, join in 3rd ch of beg
ch-6. (12 V-sts, 12 ch-3 sps)

Rnd 9: Sl st in ch-3 sp of next V-st, **beg picot** (see Special Stitches), [ch 2, dc in same sp as beg sl st, **picot** (see Special Stitches)] twice, ch 2, **dc dec** (see Stitch Guide) in next 2 dc, *(ch 2, dc, picot) 3 times in ch-3 sp of next V-st, ch 2, dc dec in next 2 dc, rep from * around, join in 3rd ch of beg ch-7.

Rnd 10: Ch 7 (counts as first tr, ch-3), *[tr in ch-2 sp between picots, ch 3] twice**, tr in next dc dec, ch 3, rep from * around, ending last rep at **, join in 4th ch of beg ch-7. (36 tr)

Rnd 11: Ch 1, sc in same st as beg ch-1, 3 sc in next ch-3 sp, [sc in next tr, 3 sc in next ch-3 sp] around, join in beg sc. (144 sc)

Rnd 12: Ch 4 (counts as first dc, ch-1), sk next sc, [dc in next sc, ch 1, sk next sc] around, join in 3rd ch of beg ch-4. (72 dc)

Rnd 13: Ch 1, sc in same st as beg ch-1, sc in next ch-1 sp, [sc in next dc, sc in next ch-1 sp] around, join in beg sc. (144 sc)

Rnd 14: Ch 1, sc in same st as beg ch-1, [ch 7, sk next 3 sc, sc in next sc] around, ch 4, join with tr in beg sc. (36 ch-7 sps)

Rnds 15–17: Ch 1, (sc, picot) in same st as beg ch-1, [ch 7, sc in next ch sp, picot] around, ch 4, join with tr in beg sc.

Rnd 18: Ch 1, (sc, picot) in same st as beg ch-1, [ch 5, 7 dc in next ch sp, ch 5, (sc, picot) in next ch-7 sp, ch 7, (sc, picot) in next ch-7 sp] around, ch 4, join with tr in beg sc. (12 groups of 7 dc)

Rnd 19: Ch 1, (sc, picot) in same st as beg ch-1, *ch 7, dc in first dc of 7-dc group, [ch 2, sk next dc, dc in next dc] 3 times, ch 7, sk next ch-5 sp, (sc, picot) in next ch sp, rep from * around, ch 4, join with tr in beg sc.

Rnd 20: Ch 1, (sc, picot) in same st as beg ch-1, *ch 7, (sc, picot) in next ch sp, ch 5, 4 dc in first ch-2 sp, 5 dc in next ch-2 sp, 4 dc in next ch-2 sp, ch 5, (sc, picot) in next ch sp, rep from * around, ch 3, join with dc in beg sc.

continued on page 42

DOILIES *in Color*

Circle of Roses

According to early traditions, white roses were used as the symbol for true love, but later the tradition changed to feature the red rose. Whether you choose to stitch Circle of Roses doily in white as shown or red, both will be a lovely addition to your home.

Circle of Roses

DESIGN BY **DONNA NICKELL**

SKILL LEVEL

◼◼◼◻
INTERMEDIATE

FINISHED SIZE
24 inches in diameter

MATERIALS
- Size 10 crochet cotton:
    400 yds white
    300 yds each fern and ecru
- Size 5/1.90mm steel crochet hook or size needed to obtain gauge
- 6mm pearl beads: 11
- Toothpicks
- Fabric glue
- Sewing needle
- Coordinating thread

GAUGE
Rose = 2¾ inches in diameter; 3 cl rnds = 1½ inches

Take time to check gauge.

PATTERN NOTES
Weave in loose ends as work progresses.

Join rounds with slip stitch as indicated unless otherwise stated.

Chain-3 counts as first double crochet as indicated unless otherwise stated.

Chain-7 counts as first double crochet and chain-4 space unless otherwise stated.

SPECIAL STITCHES

4-treble crochet cluster (4-tr cl): Yo hook twice, insert hook in indicated st, yo, draw up lp, [yo, draw through 2 lps on hook] twice, rep from * 3 times, yo, draw through all 5 lps on hook.

Beginning 4-treble crochet cluster (beg 4-tr cl): Ch 3 *(counts as first tr)*, *yo hook twice, insert hook in indicated st, yo, draw up lp, [yo, draw through 2 lps on hook] twice, rep from * twice, yo, draw through all 4 lps on hook.

Picot: Ch 4, sl st in last st made.

CENTER

Rnd 1 (RS): With ecru, ch 10, **join** *(see Pattern Notes)* in 10th ch from hook to form ring, **ch 3** *(see Pattern Notes)*, 24 dc in ring, join in 3rd ch of beg ch-3. *(25 dc)*

Rnd 2: Ch 1, sc in same st as beg ch-1, ch 25, [sc in next dc, ch 25] around, join in beg sc. *(25 ch sps)*

Rnd 3: Sl st in each of first 13 chs of next sp, ch 3, 2 dc in same ch as beg ch-3, [ch 7, 3 dc in next ch sp] around, ch 4, join with tr in 3rd ch of beg ch-3.

Rnd 4: Ch 3, 2 dc in same ch as beg ch-3, [ch 7, 3 dc in next ch-7 sp] around, ch 4, join with tr in 3rd ch of beg ch-3.

Rnd 5: Ch 3, 2 dc in same ch as beg ch-3, [ch 9, 3 dc in next ch-7 sp] around, ch 4, join with **dtr** *(see Stitch Guide)* in 3rd ch of beg ch-3.

Rnd 6: Ch 3, 2 dc in same ch as beg ch-3, [ch 11, 3 dc in next ch-9 sp] around, ch 6, join with dtr in 3rd ch of beg ch-3.

Rnd 7: **Beg 4-tr cl** *(see Special Stitches)* in same ch sp, ch 14, [**4-tr cl** *(see Special Stitches)* in next ch-11 sp, ch 14] around, join in 3rd ch of beg ch-3. *(25 cls)*

Rnd 8: Sl st in next ch sp, (beg 4-tr cl, ch 10, 4-tr cl) in same ch-14 sp as sl st, ch 3, [[4-tr cl, ch 10, 4-tr cl) in next ch-14 sp, ch 3] around, join in 3rd ch of beg ch-3. *(50 cls)*

Rnd 9: Sl st in next ch sp, (beg 4-tr cl, ch 6, 4-tr cl) in same ch sp as sl st, ch 3, 4-tr cl in next ch-3 sp, ch 3, [(4-tr cl, ch 6, 4-tr cl) in next ch-10 sp, ch 3, 4-tr cl in next ch-3 sp, ch 3] around, join in 3rd ch of beg ch-3. *(75 cls)*

Rnd 10: Sl st in next ch sp, (beg 4-tr cl, ch 4, 4-tr cl) in same ch sp as sl st, *[ch 3, 4-tr cl in next ch sp] twice, ch 3**, (4-tr cl, ch 4, 4-tr cl) in next ch sp, rep from * around, ending last rep at **, join in 3rd ch of beg ch-3. *(100 cls)*

Rnd 11: Sl st in center of next ch sp, **ch 7** *(see Pattern Notes)*, *4-tr cl in next ch sp, [ch 3, 4-tr cl in next ch sp] twice, ch 4**, dc in next ch sp, ch 4, rep from * around, ending last rep at **, join in 3rd ch of beg ch-7. *(75 cls)*

Rnd 12: Sl st in center of next ch sp, ch 7, *4-tr cl in next ch sp, ch 3, 4-tr cl in next ch sp, ch 4**, [dc in next ch sp, ch 4] twice, rep from * around, ending last rep at **, dc in next ch sp, ch 4, join in 3rd ch of beg ch-7. *(50 cls)*

Rnd 13: Sl st in center of next ch sp, ch 7, *4-tr cl in next ch sp**, [ch 4, dc in next ch sp] 3 times, ch 4, rep from * around, ending last rep at **, [ch 4, dc in next ch sp] twice, ch 4, join in 3rd ch of beg ch-7. *(25 cls)*

Rnd 14: Sl st in center of next ch sp, ch 7, [dc in next ch sp, ch 4] around, join in 3rd ch of beg ch-4. Fasten off. *(100 dc)*

Rnd 15: Join fern in any dc of rnd 14, beg 4-tr cl in same dc, sl st in next dc, [beg 4-tr cl in same dc, sl st in next dc] around, join in top of beg ch-3. Fasten off.

ROSE
MAKE 11.

Rnd 1: With white, ch 6, join in 6th ch from hook to form a ring, ch 5 *(counts as first dc, ch-2)*, [dc in ring, ch 2] 7 times, join in 3rd ch of beg ch-5. *(8 dc, 8 ch-2 sps)*

Rnd 2: (Sc, hdc, 3 dc, hdc, sc) in next ch-2 sp *(petal)* and in each rem ch-2 sp around, join in beg sc. *(8 petals)*

continued on page 43

DOILIES *in Color*

White Shamrocks

While traditional shamrocks are green with white flowers our White Shamrock doily with its Irish Rose center brings the early cool days of spring to mind all year long.

White Shamrocks

DESIGN BY **DOROTHY DRAKE**

SKILL LEVEL

EXPERIENCED

FINISHED SIZE
16½ inches in diameter

MATERIALS
- Size 10 crochet cotton:
  500 yds white
- Size 7/1.65mm steel crochet hook
  or size needed to obtain gauge
- Spray starch

GAUGE
Center = 4 inches in diameter

Take time to check gauge.

PATTERN NOTES
Weave in loose ends as work progresses.

Join rounds with slip stitch as indicated unless
   otherwise stated.

SPECIAL STITCHES
Picot: Ch 3, sl st in top of last st made.

Split double crochet decrease (split dc dec):
   Yo, insert hook in next hdc, draw up lp, yo,
   draw through 2 lps on hook, sk next 7 hdc, yo,
   insert hook in next hdc, draw up lp, yo, draw
   through 2 lps on hook, yo, draw through all
   3 lps on hook.

CENTER
Rnd 1 (RS): Ch 6, **join** (*see Pattern Notes*) in 6th
   ch from hook to form ring, ch 1, 18 sc in ring,
   join in beg sc. (*18 sc*)

Rnd 2: Ch 1, sc in same st as beg ch-1, ch 5,
   sk next 2 sc, [sc in next sc, ch 5, sk next 2 sc]
   around, join in beg sc. (*6 ch sps*)

Rnd 3: Sl st in next ch sp, ch 1, (sc, hdc, 5 dc, hdc,
   sc) in next ch-5 sp (*petal*) and in each ch-5 sp
   around, join in beg sc. (*6 petals*)

Rnd 4: Working in **back lps** (*see Stitch Guide*), [sc
   between petals, ch 5] around, join in beg sc.

Rnd 5: Sl st in next ch sp, ch 1, (sc, hdc, 7 dc, hdc,
   sc) in ch-5 sp (*petal*) and in each rem ch-5 sp
   around, join in beg sc.

Rnd 6: Working in back lps, [sc between petals,
   ch 6] around, join in beg sc.

Rnd 7: Sl st in next ch sp, ch 1, (sc, hdc, 9 dc, hdc,
   sc) in ch-6 sp (*petal*) and in each rem ch-6 sp
   around, join in beg sc.

Rnd 8: Sl st across to first dc on petal, ch 1, sc in
   same st as beg ch-1, *[ch 7, sk next 3 dc, sc in
   next dc] twice, ch 7, sc in first dc of next petal,
   rep from * 4 times, [ch 7, sk next 3 dc, sc in next
   dc] twice, ch 3, join with tr in beg sc.

Rnd 9: Ch 1, sc in same st as beg ch-1, **picot** (*see
   Special Stitches*), [ch 7, sc in next ch sp, picot]
   around, ch 3, join with tr in beg sc.

Rnd 10: Ch 1, sc in same st as beg ch-1, ch 7, [sc
   in next ch-7 sp, ch 7] around, join in beg sc.
   Fasten off.

FIRST SHAMROCK MOTIF
Rnd 1: Ch 6, join in 6th ch from hook to form
   ring, ch 1, 18 sc in ring, join in beg sc. (*18 sc*)

Rnd 2: Ch 1, sc in same sc as beg ch-1, sc in each of next 2 sc, picot, [sc in each of next 6 sc, picot] twice, sc in each of next 3 sc, join in beg sc.

Rnd 3: Ch 1, 2 sc in same sc as beg ch-1, [ch 9, sk next 2 sc after next picot, 2 sc in each of next 2 sc] twice, ch 9, sk next 2 sc after next picot, 2 sc in next sc, join in beg sc.

Rnd 4: *(Sc, hdc, 16 dc, hdc, sc) in next ch-9 sp (*petal*), sk next 2 sc**, sl st in next sc, rep from * around, ending last rep at **, join in first sc.

Rnd 5: Sl st in first dc of next petal of Shamrock, ch 5 (*counts as first dc, ch-2*), *[sk next dc, dc in next dc, ch 2] 7 times**, **dc dec** (*see Stitch Guide*) in next 2 dc, ch 2, rep from * around, ending last rep at **, dc in last dc, join in 3rd ch of beg ch-5.

Rnd 6: Sl st in next ch-2 sp, ch 1, [3 sc in next ch-2 sp, sc in next st, picot] around, join in beg sc.

Rnd 7: Sl st in next sc, ch 1, sc in same sc as beg ch-1, [ch 7, sc in center sc of 3-sc group] around, ch 4, join with tr in beg sc.

Rnd 8: Ch 1, sc in same ch sp as beg ch-1, ch 7, [sc in next ch-7 sp, ch 7] around, ch 4, join with tr in beg sc. (*24 ch sps*)

Rnd 9 (joining rnd): Ch 1, sc in same ch sp as beg ch-1, [ch 7, sc in next ch sp] 11 times, [ch 3, sc in ch-7 sp of Center, ch 3, sc in next ch-7 sp on Shamrock] 3 times, ch 7, [sc in next ch-7 sp on Shamrock, ch 7] around, join in beg sc. Fasten off.

SHAMROCK MOTIFS 2–5
Rnds 1–8: Rep rnds 1–8 of First Shamrock Motif.

Rnd 9 (joining rnd): Ch 1, sc in same ch sp as beg ch-1, [ch 7, sc in next ch sp] 11 times, join in 3rd ch sp to right of previous Shamrock, [ch 3, sc in next ch-7 sp on Center, ch 3, sc in next ch-7 sp on current Shamrock] 3 times, [ch 3, sc in next ch-7 sp on previous Shamrock, ch 3, sc in next ch-7 sp on current Shamrock] 3 times, ch 7, [sc in next ch-7 sp on current Shamrock, ch 7] around, join in beg sc. Fasten off.

continued on page 43

DOILIES *in Color*

Forget-Me-Not

Whether brightening the cool spring shade along a brookside bank or edging a summery white doily, these small dainty blue Forget-Me-Not blooms with their yellow centers will surely never be forgotten.

Forget-Me-Not

DESIGN BY **AGNES RUSSELL**

SKILL LEVEL

EASY

FINISHED SIZE
17 inches in diameter

MATERIALS
- Size 10 crochet cotton:
  325 yds white
  65 yds aqua
  20 yds yellow
- Size 8/1.50mm steel crochet hook
  or size needed to obtain gauge
- Plastic wrap-covered pinning board
- Straight pins
- Spray starch

GAUGE
4 shell rnds = 1½ inches

Take time to check gauge.

PATTERN NOTES
Weave in loose ends as work progresses.

Join rounds with slip stitch as indicated unless
  otherwise stated.

Chain-3 at beginning of row or round counts as
  first double crochet unless otherwise stated.

SPECIAL STITCHES
Beginning 3-double crochet cluster (beg 3-dc cl):
  Ch 3 *(see Pattern Notes)*, keeping last lp of each
  st on hook, work 2 dc in indicated st, yo, draw
  through all lps on hook.

3-double crochet cluster (3-dc cl): Keeping last lp
  of each st on hook, 3 dc in indicated st, yo, draw
  through all lps on hook.

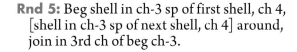

Beginning shell (beg shell): (Beg 3-dc cl, ch 3, 3-dc cl) in indicated st or sp.

Shell: (3-dc cl, ch 3, 3-dc cl) in indicated st.

Double shell: ({3-dc cl, ch 3} twice, 3-dc cl) in indicated st or sp.

Beginning double shell (beg double shell): (Beg 3-dc cl, {ch 3, 3-dc cl} twice in indicated st or sp.

Cluster decrease (cl dec): Keeping last lp of each st on hook, work 3 dc in ch sp of current shell and in ch sp of next shell, yo, draw through all lps on hook.

Shell decrease (shell dec): 3-dc cl in ch sp of next shell, ch 3, **cl dec** *(see Special Stitches)*, ch 3, 3-dc cl in ch sp of same shell as 2nd part of cl dec.

CENTER

Rnd 1 (RS): With white, ch 8, **join** *(see Pattern Notes)* in 8th ch from hook to form ring, **beg 3-dc cl** *(see Special Stitches)* in ring, ch 3, [**3-dc cl** *(see Special Stitches)* in ring, ch 3] 7 times, join in 3rd ch of beg ch-3. *(8 cls, 8 ch-3 sps)*

Rnd 2: (Beg 3-dc cl, ch 3, 3-dc cl) in first ch-3 sp, ch 3, (3-dc cl, ch 3) twice in next ch-3 sp and in each rem ch-3 sp around, join in 3rd ch of beg ch-3. *(16 cls, 16 ch-3 sps)*

Rnd 3: (Sl st, ch 1, sc) in next ch-3 sp, ch 4, [sc in next ch-3 sp, ch 4] around, join in first sc. *(16 ch-4 sps)*

Rnd 4: **Beg shell** *(see Special Stitches)* in first ch-4 sp, ch 1, [**shell** *(see Special Stitches)* in next ch-4 sp, ch 1] around, join in 3rd ch of beg ch-3. *(16 shells)*

Rnd 5: Beg shell in ch-3 sp of first shell, ch 4, [shell in ch-3 sp of next shell, ch 4] around, join in 3rd ch of beg ch-3.

Rnd 6: Beg shell in ch-3 sp of first shell, ch 4, sl st in next ch-4 sp, ch 4, [shell in ch-3 sp of next shell, ch 4, sl st in next ch-4 sp, ch 4] around, join in 3rd ch of beg ch-3.

Rnd 7: Beg shell in ch-3 sp of first shell, ch 9, [shell in ch-3 sp of shell, ch 9] around, join in 3rd ch of beg ch-3.

Rnd 8: Beg shell in ch-3 sp of first shell, ch 4, sc in next ch-9 sp, ch 4, [shell in ch-3 sp of next shell, ch 4, sc in next ch-9 sp, ch 4] around, join in 3rd ch of beg ch-3.

Rnd 9: Beg shell in ch-3 sp of first shell, ch 4, (sc, ch 3, sc) in next sc, ch 4, [shell in ch-3 sp of next shell, ch 4, (sc, ch 3, sc) in next sc, ch 4] around, join.

Rnd 10: Beg shell in ch-3 sp of first shell, ch 11, [shell in ch-3 sp of shell, ch 11] around, join in 3rd ch of beg ch-3.

Rnd 11: Beg shell in ch-3 sp of first shell, ch 5, sc in next ch-11 sp, ch 4, [shell in ch-3 sp of next shell, ch 5, sc in next ch-11 sp, ch 5] around, join in 3rd ch of beg ch-3.

Rnd 12: Beg shell in ch-3 sp of first shell, ch 6, (sc, ch 3, sc) in next sc, ch 6, [shell in ch-3 sp of shell, ch 6, (sc, ch 3, sc) in next sc, ch 6] around, join in 3rd ch of beg ch-3.

Rnd 13: Beg shell in ch-3 sp of first shell, ch 15, [shell in ch-3 sp of next shell, ch 15] around, join in 3rd ch of beg ch-3.

Rnd 14: Beg shell in ch-3 sp of first shell, ch 7, sc in next ch-15 sp, ch 7, [shell in ch-3 sp of next shell, ch 7, sc in next ch-15 sp, ch 7] around, join in 3rd ch of beg ch-3.

Rnd 15: Beg shell in ch-3 sp of first shell, ch 7, (sc, ch 5, sc) in next sc, ch 7, [shell in ch-3 sp of next shell, ch 7, (sc, ch 5, sc) in next sc, ch 7] around, join in 3rd ch of beg ch-3.

continued on page 44

DOILIES *in Color*

Orange Blossoms

In feng shui, orange is associated with the fire element and promotes conversations and good times. Orange Blossoms doily with its vibrant tones of orange is sure to bring about lots of stimulating conversation.

Orange Blossoms

DESIGN BY **JOSIE RABIER**

SKILL LEVEL

■■■□ INTERMEDIATE

FINISHED SIZE
20 inches in diameter

MATERIALS
- Size 10 crochet cotton:
  284 yds each ecru, orange and orange variegated
- Size 7/1.65mm steel crochet hook or size needed to obtain gauge

GAUGE
10 dc = 1 inch; rnds 1–3 of center motif = 2½ inches

Take time to check gauge.

PATTERN NOTES
Weave in loose ends as work progresses.

Join rounds with slip stitch as indicated unless otherwise stated.

Chain-3 at beginning of round counts as first double crochet unless otherwise stated.

CENTER MOTIF
Rnd 1 (RS): With orange, ch 8, **join** (see Pattern Notes) in 8th ch from hook to form ring, **ch 3** (see Pattern Notes), 23 dc in ring, join in top of beg ch-3. (24 dc)

Rnd 2: Ch 3, dc in same st as beg ch-3, 2 dc in each st around, join in top of beg ch-3. (48 dc)

Rnd 3: Ch 3, dc in each dc around, join in top of beg ch-3.

Rnd 4: [Ch 5, sk next dc, sl st in next dc, ch 9, sk next dc, sl st in next dc] around, sl st in same dc as beg ch-5. (12 ch-5 sps, 12 ch-9 sps)

Rnd 5: Sl st in next ch-5 sp, ch 3, 10 dc in same sp (petal), holding ch-9 sp to back, sl st in next sk dc of rnd 3, [11 dc in next ch-5 sp (petal), holding ch-9 sp to back, sl st in next sk dc of rnd 3] around, join in beg ch-3. Fasten off. (12 petals)

Rnd 6 (RS): Join orange variegated in any ch-9 sp, ch 4 (counts as first tr), 13 tr in same sp (petal), holding petal of rnd 5 forward, sl st in next sk st of rnd 3, [14 tr in next ch-9 sp (petal), holding next petal of rnd 5 forward, sl st in next sk st of rnd 3] around, join in beg ch-4. Fasten off. (12 petals)

Rnd 7: Join ecru in 3rd tr of any petal, [{ch 5, sk next 2 tr, sl st in next tr} 3 times, ch 5, sl st in 3rd tr of next petal] around, join in same st as beg ch-5. (48 ch-5 sps)

Rnd 8: Sl st in next ch-5 sp, ch 3, 4 dc in same sp, (5 dc, ch 3, 5 dc) in next ch-5 sp, 5 dc in next ch-5 sp, sl st in next ch-5 sp, [5 dc in next ch-5 sp, (5 dc, ch 3, 5 dc) in next ch-5 sp, 5 dc in next ch-5 sp, sl st in next ch-5 sp] around, join in beg ch-3. (240 dc)

Rnd 9: Sl st in 4th dc, ch 3, dc in each of next 6 dc, (3 dc, ch 3, 3 dc) in ch-3 sp, dc in each of next 7 dc, sk next 6 dc, [dc in each of next 7 dc, (3 dc, ch 3, 3 dc) in next ch-3 sp, dc in each of next 7 dc, sk next 6 dc] around, join in beg ch-3.

Rnd 10: Rep rnd 9.

Rnd 11: Sl st in 5th dc, *ch 7, sk next 5 dc, sl st in next ch-3 sp, ch 7, sk next 5 dc, sl st in next dc, ch 5, tr in same st, sk next 8 dc, tr in next dc, ch 5, sl st in same st, rep from * around, join in same st as beg ch-7. Fasten off. *(24 ch-7 sps, 12 ch-5 sps, 12 tr)*

FIRST BORDER FLOWER

Rnd 1: With orange, ch 8, join in 8th ch from hook to form ring, ch 3, 23 dc in ring, join in top of beg ch-3. *(24 dc)*

Rnd 2: [Ch 5, sk next dc, sl st in next dc, ch 9, sk next dc, sl st in next dc] around, join in same st as beg ch-5. *(6 ch-5 sps, 6 ch-9 sps)*

Rnd 3: Sl st in next ch-5 sp, ch 3, 10 dc in same sp *(petal)*, working in front of ch-9 sp, sl st in next sk dc of rnd 1, [11 dc in next ch-5 sp *(petal)*, working in front of next ch-9 sp, sl st in next sk dc of rnd 1] around, join in beg ch-3. Fasten off. *(6 petals)*

Rnd 4 (RS): Join orange variegated in ch-9 sp, ch 4 *(counts as first tr)*, 13 tr in same sp *(petal)*, holding small petal of rnd 3 to front, sl st in next sk dc of rnd 1, [14 tr in next ch-9 sp *(petal)*, holding small petal of rnd 3 to front, sl st in next sk dc of rnd 1] around, join in beg ch-3. Fasten off. *(6 petals)*

Rnds 5 & 6: Rep rnds 7 and 8 of Center Motif.

Note: *Beg joining to Center Motif in first ch-7 sp to left of (ch-5, tr) groups.*

Rnd 7: Sl st in 5th dc of 5-dc group, ch 7, sk next 5 dc, sl st in next ch-3 sp, ch 3, sl st in 4th ch of next ch-7 sp of Center Motif, ch 3, sk next 5 dc on working Border Flower, (sl st, ch 5, tr) in next dc, sl st between next 2 tr on Center Motif, sk next 8 dc on working Border Flower, (tr, ch 5, sl st) in next dc, ch 3, sl st in 4th ch of next ch-7 on Center Motif, ch 3, sl st in next ch-3 sp, [ch 7, sk next 5 dc, (sl st, ch 5, tr) in next dc, sk next 8 dc, (tr, ch 5, sl st) in next dc*, ch 7, sk next 5 dc, sl st in next ch-3 sp] around Flower, ending last rep at *. Fasten off.

continued on page 45

DOILIES *in Color*

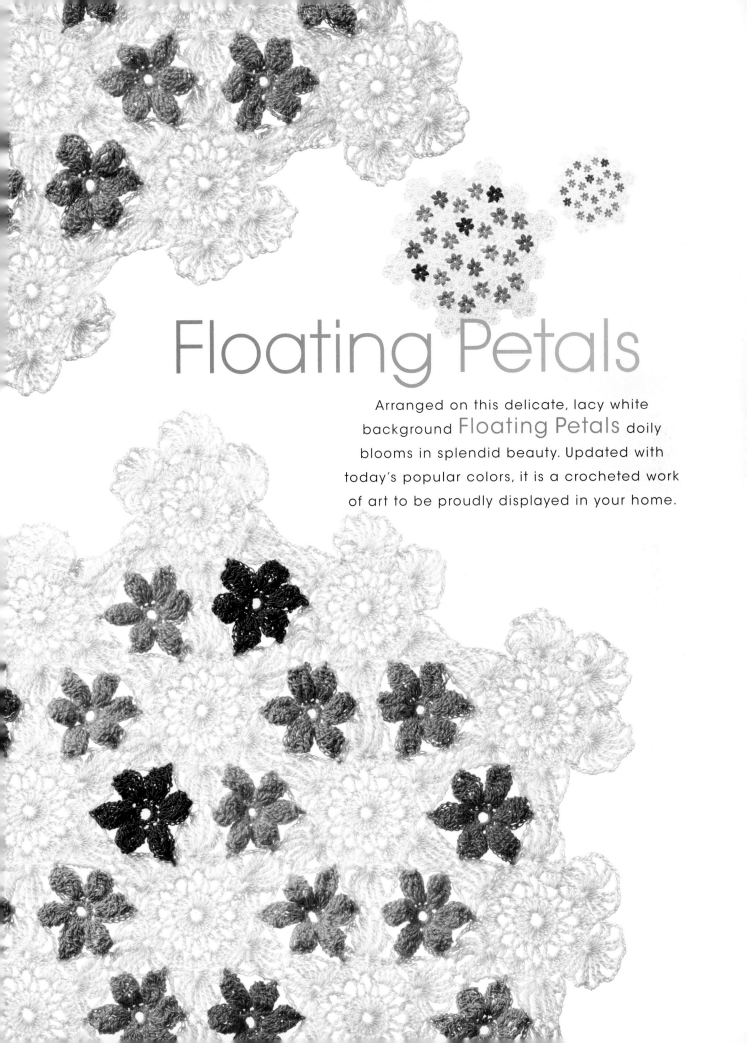

Floating Petals

Arranged on this delicate, lacy white background **Floating Petals** doily blooms in splendid beauty. Updated with today's popular colors, it is a crocheted work of art to be proudly displayed in your home.

Floating Petals

DESIGN BY **JOSIE RABIER**

SKILL LEVEL

INTERMEDIATE

FINISHED SIZE
20 inches in diameter

MATERIALS
- Size 10 crochet cotton:
  564 yds white
  282 yds each gold, orange, lilac, purple,
  pink, aqua, spring green
- Size 7/1.65mm steel crochet hook
  or size needed to obtain gauge
- Starch

GAUGE
Flower = 2½ inches in diameter;

Motif = 5½ inches in diameter; rnds 1–3 of motif
= 3 inches in diameter

Take time to check gauge.

PATTERN NOTES
Weave in loose ends as work progresses.

Join rounds with slip stitch as indicated unless
otherwise stated.

Use photo as a guide for motif and flower
placement.

Chain-3 at beginning of round counts as first
double crochet unless otherwise stated.

SPECIAL STITCHES
Popcorn (pc): 7 **dtr** *(see Stitch Guide)* in indicated
st, draw up lp, remove hook, insert hook in first
dtr of 7-dtr group, pick up dropped lp and draw
through st on hook.

V-stitch (V-st): (Dc, ch 3, dc) in indicated st.

Beginning V-stitch (beg V-st): (Ch 6, dc) in indicated st.

5-MOTIF STRIP
FIRST MOTIF
Rnd 1 (RS): With white, ch 6, **join** (see Pattern Notes) in 6th ch from hook to form a ring, **ch 3** (see Pattern Notes), 23 dc in ring, join in 3rd ch of beg ch-3. (24 dc)

Rnd 2: **Beg V-st** (see Special Stitches) in same st as joining, sk next dc, [**V-st** (see Special Stitches) in next dc, sk next dc] around, join in 3rd ch of beg ch-6. (12 V-sts)

Rnd 3: Sl st in ch-3 sp of next V-st, ch 3, 4 dc in same ch-3 sp, [5 dc in ch-3 sp of next V-st] around, join in 3rd ch of beg ch-3. (60 dc)

Rnd 4: Sl st in 3rd dc of 5-dc group, *(2 dtr, {ch 3, 2 dtr} 5 times) in 3rd dc of next 5-dc group**, sl st in 3rd dc of next 5-dc group, rep from * around, ending last rep at **, join in beg sl st. Fasten off.

2ND MOTIF
Rnds 1–3: Rep rnds 1–3 of First Motif.

Rnd 4: Sl st in 3rd dc of next 5-dc group, (2 dtr, ch 3, 2 dtr) in 3rd dc of next 5-dc group, [ch 1, sl st in 2nd ch-3 sp on previous Motif, ch 1, 2 dtr in same dc as previous dtr] 3 times, ch 3, 2 dtr in same dc as previous dtr, *sl st in 3rd dc of next 5-dc group, (2 dtr, {ch 3, 2 dtr} 5 times) in 3rd dc of next 5-dc group, rep from * around, join in beg sl st. Fasten off.

MOTIFS 3–5
Rnds 1–4: Rep rnds 1–4 of 2nd Motif.

4-MOTIF STRIP
Note: Work 1 4-Motif Strip on each side of 5-Motif Strip.

MOTIFS 1–4
Rnds 1–3: Rep rnds 1–3 of First Motif of 5-Motif Strip.

Rnd 4: Work as follows:

A. Sl st in 3rd dc of next 5-dc group, (2 dtr, ch 3, 2 dtr) in 3rd dc of next 5-dc group, [ch 1, sl st in 2nd ch-3 sp on corresponding Motif of 5-Motif Strip, ch 1, 2 dtr in same dc as previous dtr] 3 times, ch 3, 2 dtr in same dc as previous dtr;

B. sl st in 3rd dc of next 5-dc group, (2 dtr, ch 3, 2 dtr) in 3rd dc of next 5-dc group, [ch 1, sl st in 2nd ch-3 sp on corresponding Motif of 5-Motif Strip, ch 1, 2 dtr in same dc as previous dtr] 3 times, ch 3, 2 dtr in same dc as previous dtr;

C. *sl st in 3rd dc of next 5-dc group, (2 dtr, {ch 3, 2 dtr} 5 times) in 3rd dc of next 5-dc group, rep from * around, join in beg sl st. Fasten off.

For next strip of 3 Motifs, join in same manner as 4-Motif Strip, joining the 3 Motifs to the strip of 4 previous Motifs.

3-MOTIF STRIP
Note: Work 1 3-Motif Strip on rem unworked side of each 4-Motif Strip.

MOTIFS 1–4
Rnds 1–4: Rep rnds 1–4 of Motifs 1–4 of 4-Motif Strip.

FLOWER
MAKE 4 EACH ORANGE, GOLD, GREEN & PINK, 3 EACH AQUA & PURPLE & 2 LILAC.
Rnd 1: With indicated color, ch 6, join in 6th ch from hook to form a ring, ch 1, 12 hdc in ring, join in top of beg hdc. (12 hdc)

Rnd 2: [Ch 7, **pc** (see Special Stitches) in next hdc, **turn**, sl st in joining of 2 Motifs, **turn**, ch 7, sl st in next hdc on Flower, ch 7, pc in next hdc, **turn**, sl st in next sc on Motif, **turn**, ch 7, sl st in next hdc on Flower] 3 times. Fasten off. (6 petals)

Work Flowers until sps between Motifs are filled with a flower.

FINISHING
Starch lightly and press. ■

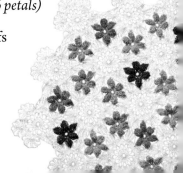

Gardenias

continued from page 7

2ND FLOWER

Rnds 1–3: Rep rnds 1–3 of First Flower.

Rnd 4: Working counterclockwise, beg shell in same ch-5 sp as join, 3 dc in next ch-5 sp, ch 1, sk 4 shells on previous Flower, sl st in ch-3 sp of next shell on previous Flower, ch 1, 3 dc in same ch-5 sp on working Flower, 3 dc in next ch-5 sp, ch 1, sl st in next ch-3 sp of previous Flower, ch 1, 3 dc in same ch-5 sp on working Flower (*working Flower joined to 2 shells of previous Flower*), [3 dc in next ch-5 sp, ch 1, sl st in next unworked ch-3 sp on rnd 12 of Doily, ch 1, 3 dc in same ch-5 sp] twice, shell in each of rem 4 ch-5 sps on working Flower, join in 3rd ch of beg ch-3. Fasten off.

3RD–14TH FLOWERS

Rnds 1–3: Rep rnds 1–3 of First Flower.

Rnd 4: Working counterclockwise, beg shell in same ch-5 sp as join, 3 dc in next ch-5 sp, ch 1, sk 2 shells on previous Flower, sl st in ch-3 sp of next shell on previous Flower, ch 1, 3 dc in same ch-5 sp on working Flower, 3 dc in next ch-5 sp, ch 1, sl st in next ch-3 sp of previous Flower, ch 1, 3 dc in same ch-5 sp on working Flower (*working Flower joined to 2 shells of previous Flower*), [3 dc in next ch-5 sp, ch 1, sl st in next unworked ch-3 sp on rnd 12 of Doily, ch 1, 3 dc in same ch-5 sp] twice, shell in each of rem 4 ch-5 sps on working Flower, join in 3rd ch of beg ch-3. Fasten off.

15TH FLOWER

Rnds 1–3: Rep rnds 1–3 of First Flower.

Rnd 4: Working counterclockwise, beg shell in same ch-5 sp as join, 3 dc in next ch-5 sp, ch 1, sk next 2 shells on previous Flower, sl st in ch-3 sp of next shell on previous Flower, ch 1, 3 dc in same ch-5 sp on working Flower, 3 dc in next ch-5 sp, ch 1, sl st in next ch-3 sp of previous Flower, ch 1, 3 dc in same ch-5 sp on

working Flower (*working Flower joined to 2 shells of previous Flower*), [3 dc in next ch-5 sp, ch 1, sl st in next unworked ch-3 sp on rnd 12 of Doily, ch 1, 3 dc in same ch-5 sp] twice, ch 1, sk 2 shells on First Flower, sl st in ch-3 sp of next shell on First Flower, ch 1, 3 dc in same ch-5 sp on working Flower, 3 dc in next ch-5 sp, ch 1, sl st in next ch-3 sp of First Flower, ch 1, 3 dc in same ch-5 sp on working Flower (*working Flower joined to 2 shells of First Flower*), shell in each of rem 2 ch-5 sps on working Flower, join in 3rd ch of beg ch-3. **Do not fasten off.**

BORDER

Rnd 1: Sl st in ch-3 sp of first shell, beg shell in same ch sp, shell in ch-3 sp of next shell, *ch 5, sk next 3 dc, tr in next dc, sk next 4 dc, tr in next dc, ch 5**, [shell in ch-3 sp of next shell] twice, rep from * around, ending last rep at **, join in 3rd ch of beg ch-3.

Rnd 2: Sl st in next ch-3 sp, beg shell in same ch sp, *ch 7, shell in ch-3 sp of next shell, ch 3, sk next 2 dc, tr in next dc, sk ch-5 sps, tr in next dc, ch 3**, shell in ch-3 sp of next shell, rep from * around, ending last rep at **, join in 3rd ch of beg ch-3.

Rnd 3: Sl st in next ch-3 sp, beg shell in same ch sp, *16 tr in next ch-7 sp, shell in ch-3 sp of next shell, ch 3, sk next ch-3 sp, sl st in each of next 2 tr, ch 3**, shell in ch-3 sp of next shell, rep from * around, ending last rep at **, join in 3rd ch of beg ch-3. (*15 pineapple bases*)

Rnd 4: Sl st in next ch-3 sp, beg shell in ch-3 sp of next shell, *dc in each of next 2 tr, [ch 1, dc in each of next 2 tr] 7 times, shell in ch-3 sp of next shell, sk ch-3 sps**, shell in ch-3 sp of next shell, rep from * around, ending last rep at **, join in 3rd ch of beg ch-3.

Rnd 5: Sl st in next ch-3 sp, beg shell in ch-3 sp of next shell, *ch 3, sl st in next ch-1 sp, [ch 5, sl st in next ch-1 sp] 6 times, ch 3**, [shell in ch-3 sp of next shell] twice, rep from * around, ending last rep at **, shell in ch-3 sp of next shell, join in 3rd ch of beg ch-3.

Rnd 6: Sl st in next ch-3 sp, beg shell in ch-3 sp of next shell, *ch 3, sl st in next ch-5 sp, [ch 5, sl st in next ch-5 sp] 5 times, ch 3**, [shell in ch-3 sp of next shell] twice, rep from * around, ending last rep at **, shell in next shell, join in 3rd ch of beg ch-3.

Rnd 7: Sl st in next ch-3 sp, beg shell in ch-3 sp of next shell, *ch 3, sl st in next ch-5 sp, [ch 5, sl st in next ch-5 sp] 4 times, ch 3, shell in ch-3 sp of next shell, ch 5**, shell in ch-3 sp of next shell, rep from * around, ending last rep at **, join in 3rd ch of beg ch-3.

Rnd 8: Sl st in next ch-3 sp, beg shell in ch-3 sp of next shell, *ch 3, sl st in next ch-5 sp, [ch 5, sl st in next ch-5 sp] 3 times, ch 3, shell in ch-3 sp of next shell, ch 5, sl st in next ch-5 sp, ch 5**, shell in ch-3 sp of next shell, rep from * around, ending last rep at **, join in 3rd ch of beg ch-3.

Rnd 9: Sl st in next ch-3 sp, beg shell in ch-3 sp of next shell, *ch 3, sl st in next ch-5 sp, [ch 5, sl st in next ch-5 sp] twice, ch 3, shell in ch-3 sp of next shell, [ch 5, sl st in next ch-5 sp] twice, ch 5**, shell in ch-3 sp of next shell, rep from * around, ending last rep at **, join in 3rd ch of beg ch-3.

Rnd 10: Sl st in next ch-3 sp, beg shell in ch-3 sp of next shell, *ch 3, sl st in next ch-5 sp, ch 5, sl st in next ch-5 sp, ch 3, shell in ch-3 sp of next shell, ch 5, sl st in next ch-5 sp, 8 tr in next ch-5 sp, sl st in next ch-5 sp, ch 5**, shell in ch-3 sp of next shell, rep from * around, ending last rep at **, join in 3rd ch of beg ch-3.

Rnd 11: Sl st in next ch-3 sp, beg shell in ch-3 sp of next shell, *ch 3, sl st in rem ch-5 sp, ch 3, shell in ch-3 sp of next shell, ch 5, sl st in next ch-5 sp, 2 tr in each of next 2 tr, [ch 3, 2 tr in each of next 2 tr] 3 times, sl st in next ch-5 sp, ch 5**, shell in ch-3 sp of next shell, rep from * around, ending last rep at **, join in 3rd ch of beg ch-3.

Rnd 12: Sl st in next ch-3 sp, beg shell in ch-3 sp of next shell, *sk next 2 ch-3 sps, shell in ch-3 sp of next shell, sk next ch-5 sp, **6-dtr dec** (*see Special Stitches*), [ch 7, sl st in next ch-3 sp, ch 7, 6-dtr cl] 3 times, sk next ch-5 sp**, shell in ch-3 sp of next shell, rep from * around, ending last rep at **, join in 3rd ch of beg ch-3. Fasten off.

FINISHING
Starch lightly and press. ∎

Irish Rose

continued from page 19

Rnd 21: Ch 1, sc in same ch sp as beg ch-1, *ch 7, (sc, picot) in next ch sp, ch 7, sc in next ch sp, [ch 7, sk next 4 dc, sc in next dc] twice, ch 7, sc in next ch sp, rep from * around, ch 4, join with tr in beg sc.

Rnd 22: Ch 1, sc in same ch sp as beg ch-1, [ch 7, sc in next ch sp] around, ch 4, join with tr in beg sc. (60 ch-7 sps)

Rnd 23: Ch 1, 6 sc in each ch sp around, join in beg sc. (360 sc)

Rnd 24: Ch 4 (counts as first dc, ch-1), sk next sc, [dc in next sc, ch 1, sk next sc] around, join in 3rd ch of beg ch-4. (180 dc)

Rnd 25: Ch 1, [sc in next dc, sc in next ch-1 sp] around, join in beg sc. (360 sc)

Rnd 26: Ch 1, sc in same st as beg ch-1, [ch 7, sk next 4 sc, sc in next sc] around, ch 4, join with tr in beg sc. (72 ch-7 sps)

Rnd 27: Beg V-st, ch 4, (sc, picot) in next ch sp, ch 4, *V-st in 4th ch of next ch-7 sp, ch 4, (sc, picot) in next ch sp, ch 4, rep from * around, join in 3rd ch of beg ch-6. (36 V-sts)

Rnd 28: Ch 4 (counts as first dc, ch-1), *(dc, ch 1) 5 times in ch-3 sp of next V-st, dc in next dc, ch 5, sc in next dc, 3 sc in ch-3 sp of next V-st, sc in next dc, ch 5**, dc in next dc, ch 1, rep from * around, ending last rep at **, join in 3rd ch of beg ch-4. (18 groups of 7 dc)

Rnd 29: Ch 6, sl st in 3rd ch from hook (counts as first dc, picot), [ch 2, dc in next dc, **ch-3 picot** (see Special Stitches)] twice, *ch 2, tr in next dc, ch-3 picot, **ch-5 picot** (see Special Stitches), ch-3 picot, tr in same dc as last tr, rep between [ ] 3 times, ch 5, sc in center sc of next 5-sc group, ch 3, sc in next sc, ch 5**, rep between [ ] 3 times, rep from * around, ending last rep at **, join in 3rd ch of beg ch-6. Fasten off.

FINISHING
Starch lightly and press. ■

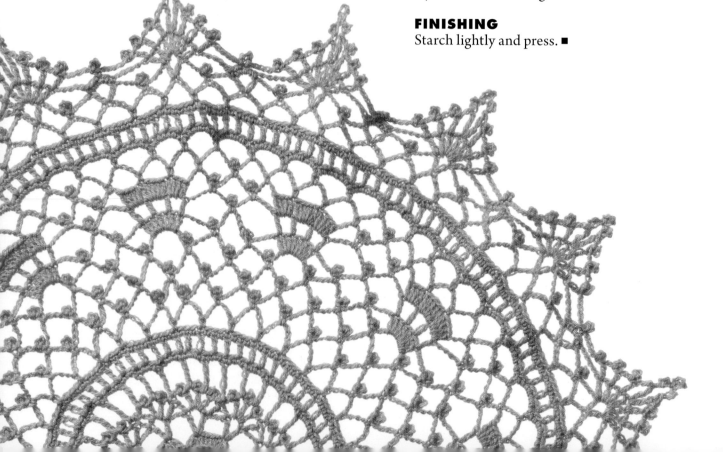

Circle of Roses
continued from page 23

Rnd 3: [Ch 4, sc in natural sp between petals] around. (8 ch-4 sps)

Rnd 4: (Sc, hdc, 5 dc, hdc, sc) in next ch-4 sp and in each rem ch-4 sp around, join in beg sc.

Rnd 5: [Ch 5, sc in natural sp between petals] around. (8 ch-5 sps)

Rnd 6: (Sc, hdc, 7 dc, hdc, sc) in next ch-5 sp and in each rem ch-5 sp around, join in beg sc.

Rnd 7: [Ch 6, sc in natural sp between petals] around.

Rnd 8: (Sc, hdc, dc, 7 tr, dc, hdc, sc) in next ch-6 sp and in each rem ch-6 sp around, join in beg sc. Fasten off.

LEAF
MAKE 12.
Rnd 1: With fern, ch 23, sc in 2nd ch from hook, ch 3, sk next 2 chs, dc in next ch, ch 3, sk next

2 chs, tr in next ch, [ch 3, sk next 2 chs, dtr in next ch] twice, ch 3, sk next 2 chs, tr in next ch, ch 3, sk next 2 chs, dc in next ch, ch 3, sk next 2 chs, (dc, ch 4, dc) in last ch, working on opposite side of foundation ch, ch 3, sk next 2 chs, dc in next ch, ch 3, sk next 2 chs, tr in next ch, [ch 3, sk next 2 chs, dtr in next ch] twice, ch 3, sk next 2 chs, tr in next ch, ch 3, sk next 2 chs, dc in next ch, ch 3, join in beg sc.

Rnd 2: Ch 3, 3 dc in next ch-3 sp, [dc in next st, **picot** (see Special Stitches), 3 dc in next ch-3 sp] 6 times, dc in next dc, picot, (3 dc, picot, 3 dc) in next ch-4 sp, [dc in next st, picot, 3 dc in next ch-3 sp] 7 times, join in 3rd ch of beg ch-3, ch 11, sc in 2nd ch from hook, sc in each of next 9 chs (stem), sl st in next st of Leaf. Fasten off.

FINISHING
Place Doily on a flat surface. Using photo as a guide, or positioning as desired, place 1 Rose and 2 Leaves at center of Doily. Place rem Leaves and Roses around outer edge of Doily as desired. Using a toothpick, place a small dot of fabric glue to hold in place. After glue is dry, tack Leaves and Roses securely in place with needle and thread. ∎

White Shamrocks
continued from page 27

LAST SHAMROCK MOTIF
Rnds 1–8: Rep rnds 1–8 of First Shamrock Motif.

Rnd 9 (joining rnd): Ch 1, sc in same ch sp as beg ch-1, [ch 7, sc in next ch sp] 8 times, join in 3rd ch sp to right of previous Shamrock, [ch 3, sc in next ch-7 sp on Center, ch 3, sc in next ch-7 sp on current Shamrock] 3 times, [ch 3, sc in next ch-7 sp on previous Shamrock, ch 3, sc in next ch-7 sp on current Shamrock] 3 times, ch 7, [sc in next ch-7 sp on current Shamrock, ch 7] 7 times, [ch 3, sc in next ch-7 sp on previous

Shamrock, ch 3, sc in next ch-7 sp on current Shamrock] 3 times, join in beg sc. Fasten off.

BORDER
Rnd 1 (RS): Join in 2nd free ch-7 sp of any Shamrock Motif, ch 2 (counts as first hdc), 5 hdc in same ch-7 sp as beg ch-2, [6 hdc in next ch-7 sp] 12 times, 3 hdc in each of next 2 ch-7 sps (last and first sps between Motifs), *[6 hdc in next ch-7 sp] 13 times, 3 hdc in each of next 2 ch-7 sps, rep from * around, join in 2nd ch of beg ch-2.

Rnd 2: Sl st in next hdc, ch 4 (counts as first dc, ch-1), *[sk next hdc, dc in next hdc, ch 1] 37 times**, sk next hdc, **split dc dec** (see Special Stitches), ch 1, rep from * around, ending last rep at **, sk next dc, dc in next hdc, join in 3rd ch of beg ch-4.

Rnd 3: Sl st in next ch-1 sp, next dc and in next ch-1 sp, ch 1, *2 sc in next ch-1 sp, sc in next dc, [2 sc in next ch-1 sp, sc in next dc] 5 times, [ch 5, **turn**, sk next 6 sc, dc, ch 5, dc in next sc, ch 5, sk next 6 sc, sc in next sc, **turn**, {4 sc, picot, 4 sc} in each of next 3 ch-5 sps, {2 sc in next ch-1 sp, sc in next dc} 7 times] 3 times, ch 5, **turn**, sk next 6 sc, dc, ch 5, dc in next sc, ch 5, sk next 6 sc, sc in next sc, **turn**, (4 sc, picot, 4 sc) in each of next 3 ch-5 sps, 2 sc in next ch-1 sp, sc in next dc, 2 sc in next ch-1 sp, sk next 2 ch-1 sps, rep from * around entire outer edge, join in beg sc. Fasten off.

FINISHING
Starch lightly and press. ■

Forget-Me-Not
continued from page 31

Rnd 16: Beg double shell *(see Special Stitches)* in ch-3 sp of first shell, ch 5, ({sc, ch 3} 3 times, sc) in next ch-5 sp, ch 5, [**double shell** *(see Special Stitches)* in ch-3 sp of next shell, ch 5, ({sc, ch 3} 3 times, sc) in next ch-5 sp, ch 5] around, join in 3rd ch of beg ch-3.

Rnd 17: Beg shell in ch-3 sp of first shell, ch 3, shell in next ch-3 sp, ch 3, {3-dc cl in next ch-3 sp, ch 3} 3 times, [{shell in next ch-3 sp, ch 3} twice, {3-dc cl in next ch-3 sp, ch 3} 3 times] around, join in 3rd ch of beg ch-3.

Rnd 18: Beg shell in ch-3 sp of first shell, ch 5, shell in ch-3 sp of next shell, ch 3, sk next ch-3 sp, {3-dc cl in next ch-3 sp, ch 3} twice, [shell in ch-3 sp of next shell, ch 5, shell in ch-3 sp of next shell, ch 3, sk next ch-3 sp, {3-dc cl in next ch-3 sp, ch 3} twice] around, join in 3rd ch of beg ch-3.

Rnd 19: Beg shell in ch-3 sp of next shell, ch 5, (sc, ch 5, sc) in next ch-5 sp, ch 5, shell in ch-3 sp of next shell, ch 3, 3-dc cl in ch-3 sp between cls, ch 3, [shell in ch-3 sp of next shell, ch 5, (sc, ch 5, sc) in next ch-5 sp, ch 5, shell in ch-3 sp of next shell, ch 3, 3-dc cl in ch-3 sp between cls, ch 3] around, join in 3rd ch of beg ch-3.

Rnd 20: Beg shell in ch-3 sp of next shell, ch 5, (tr, {ch 1, tr} 4 times) in center ch-5 sp, ch 5, shell in ch-3 sp of next shell, ch 3, sl st in top of next 3-dc cl, ch 3, [shell in ch-3 sp of next shell, ch 5, (tr, {ch 1, tr} 4 times) in center ch-5 sp, ch 5, shell in ch-3 sp of next shell, ch 3, sl st in top of next 3-dc cl, ch 3] around, join in 3rd ch of beg ch-3.

Rnd 21: (Sl st, beg 3-dc cl) in ch-3 sp of first shell, *ch 5, 3-dc cl in next ch-1 sp, [ch 3, 3-dc cl in next ch-1 sp] 3 times, ch 5**, **shell dec** *(see Special Stitches)*, rep from * around, ending last rep at **, 3-dc cl in ch sp of next shell, **cl dec** *(see Special Stitches)*, join in top of beg 3-dc cl. Fasten off.

FIRST FLOWER CENTER
Row 1 (RS): Join maize in first ch-3 sp to the left of any ch-5 sp on rnd 21, *ch 4 *(counts as first dc, ch-1)*, ({dc, ch 1} 4 times, ch 3, sl st) in same ch-3 sp as beg ch-4**, sl st in next ch-3 sp, rep from * twice, ending last rep at **. Fasten off. *(3 groups of 5 ch-1 sps)*

FLOWER CENTERS 2–16
Row 1: Rep row 1 of First Flower Center.

FIRST FLOWER PETALS
Rnd 1 (RS): Join aqua in first ch-1 sp in any group of 5 ch-1 sps on Flower Center, ch 1, (sc, 3 dc, sc) in each of next 5 ch-1 sps, **turn**, *(first petal is now to left)*, join in beg sc. Fasten off.

REM FLOWER PETALS
Rnd 1: Rep rnd 1 of First Flower Petal in each group of 5 ch-1 sps around outer edge. *(16 groups of 3 flowers; total 48 flowers)*

FINISHING
Adjust flowers so that center flower is on top of the flowers at each side. Pin doily to board in each center ch-3 sp of rnd 21. Saturate with spray starch. Allow to dry completely. ■

Orange Blossoms
continued from page 35

BORDER FLOWERS 2–11
Rnds 1–6: Rep rnds 1–6 of First Border Flower.

Rnd 7: Sl st across to 5th dc of 5-dc group, ch 7, sk next 5 dc, sl st in next ch-3 sp, ch 3, sl st in 4th ch of ch-7 sp of Center Motif, ch 3, sk next 5 dc on working Border Flower, sl st in next dc, ch 5, tr in same dc as ch-5, sl st between 2 tr on Center Motif, sk next 8 dc on working Border Flower, tr in next dc, ch 5, sl st in same dc, ch 3, sl st in 4th ch of next ch-7 on Center Motif, ch 3, sl st in ch-3 sp, ch 3, sl st in 4th ch of next ch-7 sp on previous Border Flower, ch 3, sk next 5 dc, sl st in next dc, ch 5, tr in same dc, sl st between tr sts on previous Border Flower, sk next 8 dc on working Border Flower, tr in next dc, ch 5, sl st in same dc as last tr, ch 3, sl st in 4th ch of next ch-7 sp on previous Border Flower, ch 3, sl st in next ch-3 sp, *ch 7, sk next 5 dc, sl st in next dc, ch 5, tr in same dc, sk next 8 dc, tr in next dc, ch 5, sl st in same dc**, ch 7, sk next 5 dc, sl st in next ch-3 sp, rep from * around Border Flower, ending last rep at **. Fasten off.

BORDER FLOWER 12
Rnds 1–6: Rep rnds 1–6 of First Border Flower.

Rnd 7: Work as follows:

A. Ch 3, sl st in 4th ch of next ch-7 sp on First Border Flower, ch 3, sk next 5 dc, sl st in next ch-3 sp, ch 3, sl st in 4th ch of ch-7 sp of Center Motif;

B. ch 3, sk next 5 dc on working Border Flower, sl st in next dc, ch 5, tr in same dc as ch-5;

C. sl st between 2 tr on Center Motif;

D. sk next 8 dc on working Border Flower, tr in next dc, ch 5, sl st in same dc;

E. ch 3, sl st in 4th ch of next ch-7 on Center Motif, ch 3, sl st in next ch-3 sp on Center Motif;

F. ch 3, sl st in 4th ch of next ch-7 sp on previous Border Flower, ch 3, sk next 5 dc, sl st in next dc, ch 5, tr in same dc, sl st between tr sts on previous Border Flower;

G. sk next 8 dc on working Border Flower, tr in next dc, ch 5, sl st in same dc as last tr, ch 3;

H. sl st in 4th ch of next ch-7 sp on previous Border Flower, ch 3, sl st in next ch-3 sp on working Border Flower;

I. [ch 7, sk next 5 dc, sl st in next dc, ch 5, tr in same dc, sk next 8 dc, tr in next dc, ch 5, sl st in same dc*, ch 7, sk next 5 dc, sl st in next ch-3 sp] 3 times, ending last rep at *;

J. ch 3, sl st in 4th ch of next ch-7 sp on First Border Flower, ch 3, sk next 5 dc, sl st in next dc, ch 5, tr in same dc, sl st between tr sts on First Border Flower;

K. sk next 8 dc on working Border Flower, tr in next dc, ch 5, join in same st as beg ch-3. Fasten off.

FINISHING
With WS facing, starch and press Doily lightly. ∎

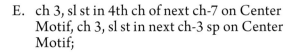

STITCH GUIDE

Need help? ▶ **StitchGuide.com** • ILLUSTRATED GUIDES • HOW-TO VIDEOS

STITCH ABBREVIATIONS

beg	begin/begins/beginning
bpdc	back post double crochet
bpsc	back post single crochet
bptr	back post treble crochet
CC	contrasting color
ch(s)	chain(s)
ch-	refers to chain or space previously made (i.e., ch-1 space)
ch sp(s)	chain space(s)
cl(s)	cluster(s)
cm	centimeter(s)
dc	double crochet (singular/plural)
dc dec	double crochet 2 or more stitches together, as indicated
dec	decrease/decreases/decreasing
dtr	double treble crochet
ext	extended
fpdc	front post double crochet
fpsc	front post single crochet
fptr	front post treble crochet
g	gram(s)
hdc	half double crochet
hdc dec	half double crochet 2 or more stitches together, as indicated
inc	increase/increases/increasing
lp(s)	loop(s)
MC	main color
mm	millimeter(s)
oz	ounce(s)
pc	popcorn(s)
rem	remain/remains/remaining
rep(s)	repeat(s)
rnd(s)	round(s)
RS	right side
sc	single crochet (singular/plural)
sc dec	single crochet 2 or more stitches together, as indicated
sk	skip/skipped/skipping
sl st(s)	slip stitch(es)
sp(s)	space(s)/spaced
st(s)	stitch(es)
tog	together
tr	treble crochet
trtr	triple treble
WS	wrong side
yd(s)	yard(s)
yo	yarn over

YARN CONVERSION

OUNCES TO GRAMS	GRAMS TO OUNCES
1 ...... 28.4	25 ...... ⅞
2 ...... 56.7	40 ...... 1⅔
3 ...... 85.0	50 ...... 1¾
4 ...... 113.4	100 ...... 3½

UNITED STATES		UNITED KINGDOM
sl st (slip stitch)	=	sc (single crochet)
sc (single crochet)	=	dc (double crochet)
hdc (half double crochet)	=	htr (half treble crochet)
dc (double crochet)	=	tr (treble crochet)
tr (treble crochet)	=	dtr (double treble crochet)
dtr (double treble crochet)	=	ttr (triple treble crochet)
skip	=	miss

Reverse single crochet (reverse sc): Ch 1, sk first st, working from left to right, insert hook in next st from front to back, draw up lp on hook, yo and draw through both lps on hook.

Chain (ch): Yo, pull through lp on hook.

Single crochet (sc): Insert hook in st, yo, pull through st, yo, pull through both lps on hook.

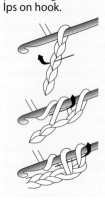

Double crochet (dc): Yo, insert hook in st, yo, pull through st, [yo, pull through 2 lps] twice.

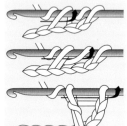

Front loop (front lp) Back loop (back lp)

Front Loop   Back Loop

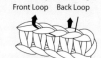

Front post stitch (fp): Back post stitch (bp): When working post st, insert hook from right to left around post of st on previous row.

Back   Front

Post of Stitch

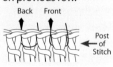

Half double crochet (hdc): Yo, insert hook in st, yo, pull through st, yo, pull through all 3 lps on hook.

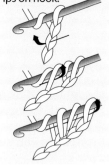

Double treble crochet (dtr): Yo 3 times, insert hook in st, yo, pull through st, [yo, pull through 2 lps] 4 times.

Slip stitch (sl st): Insert hook in st, pull through both lps on hook.

Chain color change (ch color change) Yo with new color, draw through last lp on hook.

Double crochet color change (dc color change) Drop first color, yo with new color, draw through last 2 lps of st.

Treble crochet (tr): Yo twice, insert hook in st, yo, pull through st, [yo, pull through 2 lps] 3 times.

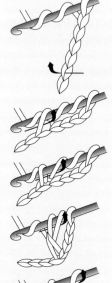

Single crochet decrease (sc dec): (Insert hook, yo, draw lp through) in each of the sts indicated, yo, draw through all lps on hook.

Example of 2-sc dec

Half double crochet decrease (hdc dec): (Yo, insert hook, yo, draw lp through) in each of the sts indicated, yo, draw through all lps on hook.

Example of 2-hdc dec

Double crochet decrease (dc dec): (Yo, insert hook, yo, draw lp through, yo, draw through 2 lps on hook) in each of the sts indicated, yo, draw through all lps on hook.

Example of 2-dc dec

Treble crochet decrease (tr dec): Holding back last lp of each st, tr in each of the sts indicated, yo, pull through all lps on hook.

Example of 2-tr dec

Metric Conversion Charts

METRIC CONVERSIONS

yards	x	.9144	=	metres (m)
yards	x	91.44	=	centimetres (cm)
inches	x	2.54	=	centimetres (cm)
inches	x	25.40	=	millimetres (mm)
inches	x	.0254	=	metres (m)

centimetres	x	.3937	=	inches
metres	x	1.0936	=	yards

INCHES INTO MILLIMETRES & CENTIMETRES (Rounded off slightly)

inches	mm	cm	inches	cm	inches	cm	inches	cm
1/8	3	0.3	5	12.5	21	53.5	38	96.5
1/4	6	0.6	5 1/2	14	22	56	39	99
3/8	10	1	6	15	23	58.5	40	101.5
1/2	13	1.3	7	18	24	61	41	104
5/8	15	1.5	8	20.5	25	63.5	42	106.5
3/4	20	2	9	23	26	66	43	109
7/8	22	2.2	10	25.5	27	68.5	44	112
1	25	2.5	11	28	28	71	45	114.5
1 1/4	32	3.2	12	30.5	29	73.5	46	117
1 1/2	38	3.8	13	33	30	76	47	119.5
1 3/4	45	4.5	14	35.5	31	79	48	122
2	50	5	15	38	32	81.5	49	124.5
2 1/2	65	6.5	16	40.5	33	84	50	127
3	75	7.5	17	43	34	86.5		
3 1/2	90	9	18	46	35	89		
4	100	10	19	48.5	36	91.5		
4 1/2	115	11.5	20	51	37	94		

KNITTING NEEDLES CONVERSION CHART

Canada/U.S.	0	1	2	3	4	5	6	7	8	9	10	10½	11	13	15
Metric (mm)	2	2.25	2.75	3.25	3.5	3.75	4	4.5	5	5.5	6	6.5	8	9	10

CROCHET HOOKS CONVERSION CHART

Canada/U.S.	1/B	2/C	3/D	4/E	5/F	6/G	8/H	9/I	10/J	10½/K	N
Metric (mm)	2.25	2.75	3.25	3.5	3.75	4.25	5	5.5	6	6.5	9.0

 *Doilies in Color* is published by Annie's, 306 East Parr Road, Berne, IN 46711. Printed in USA. Copyright © 2011, 2015 Annie's. All rights reserved. This publication may not be reproduced in part or in whole without written permission from the publisher.

RETAIL STORES: If you would like to carry this publication or any other Annie's publications, visit AnniesWSL.com.

Every effort has been made to ensure that the instructions in this publication are complete and accurate. We cannot, however, take responsibility for human error, typographical mistakes or variations in individual work. Please visit AnniesCustomerService.com to check for pattern updates.

ISBN: 978-1-59635-398-5
13 14 15 16 17 18 19